三十八計

Thirty Six Stratagems

A Chinese Strategy Classic

 **DRAGON READER**

Bilingual Edition
Chinese/English Side-by-Side

Bilingual Study Edition © Copyright 2016 Dragon Reader

Table of Contents

上屋抽梯　Remove the ladder when the enemy has ascended to the roof

樹上開花　Deck the tree with false blossoms

反客為主　Make the host and the guest exchange roles

Chapter 6: 敗戰計 Desperate Stratagems　　page 35

美人計　The Beauty Trap (Honeypot)

空城計　The empty fort strategy

反間計　Let the enemy's own spy sow discord in the enemy camp

苦肉計　Inflict injury on oneself to win the enemy's trust

連環計　Chain stratagems

走為上　If all else fails, retreat

Dragon Reader Classical Chinese Study Guide
page 41

Chapter 1: 勝戰計 Winning Stratagems

瞞天過海

Mán tiān guò hǎi

Deceive the heavens to cross the ocean

Mask your real goals, by using the ruse of a fake goal, until the real goal is achieved. Tactically, this is known as an 'open feint': in front of everyone, you point west, when your goal is actually in the east.

圍魏救趙

Wéi Wèi jiù Zhào

Besiege Wèi to rescue Zhào

When the enemy is too strong to be attacked directly, then attack something he holds dear. Know that he cannot be superior in all things. Somewhere there is a gap in the armour, a weakness that can be attacked instead. The idea here is to avoid a head on battle with a strong enemy, and instead strike at his weakness elsewhere. This will force the strong enemy to retreat in order to support his weakness. Battling against the now tired and low-morale enemy will give a much higher chance of success.

借刀殺人

Jiè dāo shā rén

Kill with a borrowed sword

Attack using the strength of another (in a situation where using one's own strength is not favourable). Trick an ally into attacking him, bribe an official to turn traitor, or use the enemy's own strength against him. The idea here is to cause damage to the enemy by getting a 3rd party to do the deed.

以逸待勞

Yǐ yì dài láo

Wait at leisure while the enemy labors

It is an advantage to choose the time and place for battle. In this way you know when and where the battle will take place, while your enemy does not. Encourage your enemy to expend his energy in futile quests while you conserve your strength. When he is exhausted and confused, you attack with energy and purpose. The idea is to have your troops well-prepared for battle, in the same time that the enemy is rushing to fight against you. This will give your troops a huge advantage in the upcoming battle, of which you will get to select the time and place.

趁火打劫

Chèn huǒ dǎ jié

Loot a burning house

When a country is beset by internal conflicts, when disease and famine ravage the population, when corruption and crime are rampant, then it will be unable to deal with an outside threat. This is the time to attack. Keep gathering internal information about an enemy. If the enemy is currently in its weakest state ever, attack it without mercy and totally destroy it to prevent future troubles.

聲東擊西

Shēng dōng jī xī

Make a sound in the east, then strike in the west

In any battle the element of surprise can provide an overwhelming advantage. Even when face to face with an enemy, surprise can still be employed by attacking where he least expects it. To do this you must create an expectation in the enemy's mind through the use of a feint. The idea here is to get the enemy to focus his forces in a location, and then attack elsewhere which would be weakly defended.

Chapter 2: 敵戰計 Enemy Dealing Stratagems

無中生有

Wú zhōng shēng yǒu

Create something from nothing

A plain lie. Make somebody believe there was something when there is in fact nothing. One method of using this strategy is to create an illusion of something's existence, while it does not exist. Another method is to create an illusion that something does not exist, while it does.

明修棧道,暗渡陳倉

Míng xiū zhàn dào, àn dù chén cāng

Openly repair the gallery roads, but sneak through the passage of Chencang

Deceive the enemy with an obvious approach that will take a very long time, while surprising him by taking a shortcut and sneak up to him. As the enemy concentrates on the decoy, he will miss you sneaking up to him. This tactic is an extension of the "Make a sound in the east, then strike in the west" tactic. But instead of simply spreading misinformation to draw the enemy's attention, physical baits are used to increase the enemy's certainty on the misinformation. These baits must be easily seen by the enemy, to ensure that they draw the enemy's attention. At the same time, the baits must act as if they are meant to do what they were falsely doing, to avoid drawing the enemy's suspicion.

隔岸觀火

Gé àn guān huǒ

Watch the fires burning across the river

Delay entering the field of battle until all the other players have become exhausted fighting amongst themselves. Then go in at full strength and pick up the pieces.

笑裏藏刀

Xiào lǐ cáng dāo

Hide a knife behind a smile

Charm and ingratiate yourself to your enemy. When you have gained his trust, move against him in secret.

李代桃僵

Lǐ dài táo jiāng

Sacrifice the plum tree to preserve the peach tree

There are circumstances in which you must sacrifice short-term objectives in order to gain the long-term goal. This is the scapegoat strategy whereby someone else suffers the consequences so that the rest do not.

順手牽羊

Shùn shǒu qiān yang

Take the opportunity to pilfer a goat

While carrying out your plans be flexible enough to take advantage of any opportunity that presents itself, however small, and avail yourself of any profit, however slight.

Chapter 3: 攻戰計 Attacking Stratagems

打草驚蛇

Dá cǎo jīng shé

Stomp the grass to scare the snake

Do something unaimed, but spectacular ("hitting the grass") to provoke a response of the enemy ("startle the snake"), thereby giving away his plans or position, or just taunt him. Do something unusual, strange, and unexpected as this will arouse the enemy's suspicion and disrupt his thinking. More widely used as "[Do not] startle the snake by hitting the grass". An imprudent act will give your position or intentions away to the enemy.

借屍還魂

Jiè shī huán hún

Borrow a corpse to resurrect the soul

Take an institution, a technology, a method, or even an ideology that has been forgotten or discarded and appropriate it for your own purpose. Revive something from the past by giving it a new purpose or bring to life old ideas, customs, or traditions and reinterpret them to fit your purposes.

調虎離山

Diào hǔ lí shān

Entice the tiger to leave its mountain lair

Never directly attack an opponent whose advantage is derived from its position. Instead lure him away from his position thus separating him from his source of strength.

欲擒故縱

Yù qín gū zòng

In order to capture, one must let loose

Cornered prey will often mount a final desperate attack. To prevent this you let the enemy believe he still has a chance for freedom. His will to fight is thus dampened by his desire to escape. When in the end the freedom is proven a falsehood the enemy's morale will be defeated and he will surrender without a fight.

抛砖引玉

Pāo zhuān yǐn yù

Tossing out a brick to get a jade gem

Bait someone by making him believe he gains something or just make him react to it ("toss out a brick") and obtain something valuable from him in return ("get a jade gem").

擒賊擒王

Qín zéi qín wáng

Defeat the enemy by capturing their chief

If the enemy's army is strong but is allied to the commander only by money, superstition or threats, then take aim at the leader. If the commander falls the rest of the army will disperse or come over to your side. If, however, they are allied to the leader through loyalty then beware, the army can continue to fight on after his death out of vengeance.

Chapter 4: 混戰計 Chaos Stratagems

釜底抽薪

Fǔ dǐ chōu xīn

Remove the firewood from under the pot

Take out the leading argument or asset of someone; "steal someone's thunder". This is the very essence of indirect approach: instead of attacking enemy's fighting forces, the attacks are directed against his ability to wage war.

渾水摸魚

Hún shuǐ mō yú

Disturb the water and catch a fish

Create confusion and use this confusion to further your own goals.

金蟬脫殼

Jīn chán tuō qiào

Slough off the cicada's golden shell

Mask yourself. Either leave one's distinctive traits behind, thus becoming inconspicuous, or masquerade as something or someone else. This strategy is mainly used to escape from enemy of superior strength.

關門捉賊

Guān mén zhuō zéi

Shut the door to catch the thief

To capture your enemy, or more generally in fighting wars, to deliver the final blow to your enemy, you must plan prudently if you want to succeed. Do not rush into action. Before you "move in for the kill", first cut off your enemy's escape routes, and cut off any routes through which outside help can reach them.

遠交近攻

Yuǎn jiāo jìn gong

Befriend a distant state while attacking a neighbor

It is known that nations that border each other become enemies while nations separated by distance and obstacles make better allies. When you are the strongest in one field, your greatest threat is from the second strongest in your field, not the strongest from another field.

假道伐虢

Jiǎ dào fá Guó

Obtain safe passage to conquer the State of Guo

Borrow the resources of an ally to attack a common enemy. Once the enemy is defeated, use those resources to turn on the ally that lent you them in the first place.

Chapter 5: 並戰計 Proximate Stratagems

偷梁換柱

Tōu liáng huàn zhù

Replace the beams with rotten timbers

Disrupt the enemy's formations, interfere with their methods of operations, change the rules in which they are used to follow, go contrary to their standard training. In this way you remove the supporting pillar, the common link that makes a group of men an effective fighting force.

指桑罵槐

Zhǐ sāng mà huái

Point at the mulberry tree while cursing the locust tree

To discipline, control, or warn others whose status or position excludes them from direct confrontation; use analogy and innuendo. Without directly naming names, those accused cannot retaliate without revealing their complicity.

假痴不癲

Jiǎ chī bù diān

Feign madness but keep your balance

Hide behind the mask of a fool, a drunk, or a madman to create confusion about your intentions and motivations. Lure your opponent into underestimating your ability until, overconfident, he drops his guard. Then you may attack.

上屋抽梯

Shàng wū chōu tī

Remove the ladder when the enemy has ascended to the roof

With baits and deceptions, lure your enemy into treacherous terrain. Then cut off his lines of communication and avenue of escape. To save himself, he must fight both your own forces and the elements of nature.

樹上開花

Shù shàng kāi huā

Deck the tree with false blossoms

Tying silk blossoms on a dead tree gives the illusion that the tree is healthy. Through the use of artifice and disguise, make something of no value appear valuable; of no threat appear dangerous; of no use appear useful.

反客為主

Fǎn kè wéi zhǔ

Make the host and the guest exchange roles

Usurp leadership in a situation where you are normally subordinate. Infiltrate your target. Initially, pretend to be a guest to be accepted, but develop from inside and become the owner later.

Chapter 6: 敗戰計 Desperate Stratagems

Měi rén jì

The beauty trap (Honeypot)

Send your enemy beautiful women to cause discord within his camp. This strategy can work on three levels. First, the ruler becomes so enamoured with the beauty that he neglects his duties and allows his vigilance to wane. Second, other males at court will begin to display aggressive behaviour that inflames minor differences hindering co-operation and destroying morale. Third, other females at court, motivated by jealousy and envy, begin to plot intrigues further exacerbating the situation.

空城計

Kōng chéng jì

The empty fort strategy

When the enemy is superior in numbers and your situation is such that you expect to be overrun at any moment, then drop all pretense of military preparedness, act calmly and taunt the enemy, so that the enemy will think you have a huge ambush hidden for them. It works best by acting calm and at ease when your enemy expects you to be tense. This ploy is only successful if in most cases you do have a powerful hidden force and only sparsely use the empty fort strategy.

反間計

Fǎn jiàn jì

Let the enemy's own spy sow discord in the enemy camp

Undermine your enemy's ability to fight by secretly causing discord between him and his friends, allies, advisors, family, commanders, soldiers, and population. While he is preoccupied settling internal disputes, his ability to attack or defend, is compromised.

苦肉計

Kǔ ròu jì

Inflict injury on oneself to win the enemy's trust

Pretending to be injured has two possible applications. In the first, the enemy is lulled into relaxing his guard since he no longer considers you to be an immediate threat. The second is a way of ingratiating yourself to your enemy by pretending the injury was caused by a mutual enemy.

連環計

Lián huán jì

Chain stratagems

In important matters, one should use several stratagems applied simultaneously after another as in a chain of stratagems. Keep different plans operating in an overall scheme; however, in this manner if any one strategy fails, then the chain breaks and the whole scheme fails.

走為上

Zǒu wéi shàng

If all else fails, retreat

If it becomes obvious that your current course of action will lead to defeat, then retreat and regroup. When your side is losing, there are only three choices remaining: surrender, compromise, or escape. Surrender is complete defeat, compromise is half defeat, but escape is not defeat. As long as you are not defeated, you still have a chance. This is the most famous of the stratagems, immortalized in the form of a Chinese idiom: "Of the Thirty-Six Stratagems, fleeing is best" (三十六计，走为上计).

Dragon Reader
Classical Chinese Quick Study Guide

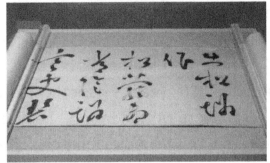

Introduction

Classical Chinese 文言文, is also known as Literary Chinese. It is both poetic and sophisticated, and may be one of the most compact languages in the world. While literary Chinese has been used for approximately 2,500 years, Classical Chinese "classic texts" were written from 5th century BC to 2nd century AD. This period roughly coincides from the end of the Spring and Autumn period through the end of the Han Dynasty. This unique form of Chinese comes from a long tradition of written Chinese, and does not correspond to spoken Chinese. In fact, many believe that Classical Chinese was never spoken at all, believing it was strictly a written form of communication. Native speakers of Chinese, Japanese and Korean can interpret the texts, though their pronunciations of the characters will differ. This tradition of formal Classical Chinese, similar to Latin in the West, is no longer widely used, being replaced with written vernacular modern Chinese. However, the rich heritage of Classical Chinese texts continue to influence the world with some of the greatest classic writing the world has produced.

Chinese speakers with at least a middle or high school education can read and interact with basic Classical Chinese. This is because it is part of the middle school and high school curriculum in China, and also tested in the critically important college entrance exam. Many of the classical texts continue to hold very strong cultural influence in China.

Characteristics of Classical Chinese

Concise and compact

Classical Chinese is generally more concise and compact than modern Chinese. A different vocabulary and set of unique characters is used. In some cases, Classical Chinese may use half the number of characters as modern Chinese to relay the same amount of information.

No Punctuation

Classical Chinese traditionally employed no punctuation markings. The texts utilized characters to represents punctuation marks, such as sentence endings and quotation marks.

Text Direction

The Chinese language is traditionally read from top to bottom in a column, with the columns flowing from left to right.

One syllable words

While modern Chinese utilizes two syllable words, Classical Chinese uses mostly one syllable words.

More pronouns

Classical Chinese has more pronouns than modern Chinese. This includes more pronouns for honorific situations and different grammatical uses.

Implied omission

Classical Chinese often drops subjects, verbs and objects that are implied or not necessary.

Words not restricted to set parts of speech

Words in Classical Chinese are not restricted to set parts of speech. A given word can act as a verb, adjective or a noun in different sentences. This process is called conversion, and occurs in English as well (example: "I love him", a verb - "his love", a noun).

More particles

Classical Chinese utilizes many particles for sentence endings and questions.

Reversed Word Order

Multiple character words in Classical Chinese can often reverse the order, retaining the meaning regardless of the reversal of the characters. For example, the word 饶恕 (ráoshù, "to forgive") may easily appear as 恕饶 while retaining the same meaning.

Examples of Distinct and Common Classical Chinese Characters

子 zǐ This character is used to address a teacher or master. Many of the famous authors will have this title given to them, such of Confucius or Mencius.

曰 yue   A character that means "to say" in classical Chinese.

乎 hū Marks a question, similar to the modern 吗。

也 yě A sentence ending final particle showing strong affirmation. Essentially this character is a strong period.

亦 yì Yi can be translated as "also". It does not add a lot of meaning to the sentence in many cases.

之 zhī   Often seen as the classical form of the modern possessive particle 的, but also acts as a third person pronoun.

君子 jūn zǐ Roughly translated as "gentlemanly", this references the upright individual that lives life correctly.

子曰 zǐ yue "The master says" refers to the words of the sage. In many cases, this refers to Confucius.

其 qí Third person pronoun for his/her/theirs.

焉 yān Thereupon, how?, why?, where?

吾 wú 1st person pronoun I/my, compare to modern 我

汝 rǔ 2nd person pronoun you, compare to modern 你

爾/尔 ěr 2nd person pronoun you, compare to modern 你

矣 yǐ Classical final particle of completed action, compare to modern 了

与/與 yǔ and / with / as with

Most Important Chinese Classical Texts

The most important and culturally influential Chinese classical texts include the texts from Confucianism, Daoism, Mohism, Legalism, Military, Chinese history and poetry. From these categories, 9 specific books in particular were used as the center of the Imperial Examination educational system. The exam focused on rote learning and memorization of these classic texts. These books have come to be known as the "Five Classics" and the "Four Books" 四书五经.

Five Classics:

1. 易经 I Ching, or Book of Changes. A divination manual for folk religion and fortunes.
2. 诗经 Classic of Poetry, collection of classic poems, songs, festival songs and eulogies.
3. 礼经 Classic of Rites

4. 尚书 Classic of History, history and speeches from rulers of the early Zhou period.
5. 春秋 Spring and Autumn Annals, historical records from Confucius' native state.

Four Books:

1. 论域 Analects of Confucius, teachings of Confucius written by his disciples.
2. 孟子 Mencius, political dialogues of the philosopher Mencius.
3. 中庸 Doctrine of the Mean, Confucian teaching from the Classic of Rites
4. 大学 Great Learning, Confucian teaching from the Classic of Rites

<u>Other Major Classical Texts:</u>

1. 道德经 Dao De Jing, primary Daoist philosophical text
2. 庄子 Zhuangzi, Daoist philosopher's teachings
3. 孙子兵法 The Art of War, military science by Sun Tzu
4. 唐诗 300 Tang Poems, classic collection of Tang Poetry
5. 列子 Liezi, Daoist philosopher's teachings

Recommended Resources to Help Study Classical Chinese

Gregory Chiang: Language of the Dragon: A Classical Chinese Reader, Volume 1 and 2

Michael A. Fuller: An introduction to Literary Chinese, Harvard Univ. Asia Center

Paul Rouzer: A New Practical Primer of Literary Chinese

Harold Shadick: A First Course in Literary Chinese

Wang Li 王力, Classical Chinese 古代漢語

BLCU's Classical Chinese Textbook series 古代汉语课本 by 徐宗才

100 Most Frequent Classical Chinese Characters

1 　之　zhi1　(classical form of 的)/(subor. part.)/him/her/it

2 　不　bu4/bu2　(negative prefix)/not/no

3 　一　yi1　one/1/single/a(n)

4 　人　ren2　man/person/people

5 　以　yi3　to use/according to/so as to/in order to/by/with/because

6 　有　you3　to have/there is/there are/to exist/to be

7 　了　le/liao3/liao4　(modal particle intensifying preceding clause)/(completed action marker), to know/to understand/to know, clear, look afar from a high place

8 　为　wei2/wei4　act as/take...to be/to be/to do/to serve as/to become, because of/for/to

9   道   dao4
direction/way/method/road/path/principle /truth/reason/skill/ method/Tao (of Taoism)/a measure word/to say/to speak/to talk

10   是   shi4   is/are/am/yes/to be

11   子   zi3/zi 11p.m.-1a.m./1[st]earthly branch/child/midnight/son/child/ seed/egg/small thing, (noun suff.)

12   的   de/di2/di4   (possessive particle)/of, really and truly, aim/clear

13   来   lai2   to come

14   大   da4/dai4
big/huge/large/major/great/wide/deep/old est/eldest, doctor

15   也   ye3   also/too

16   十   shi2   ten/10

17   其   qi2   his/her/its/theirs/that/such/it (refers to something preceding it)

18   上   shang4   on/on top/upon/first (of two parts)/previous or last (week,

etc.)/upper/higher/above/previous/to climb/to go into/above/to go up

19   二   er4   two/2

20   而   er2   and/as well as/but (not)/yet (not)/(shows causal relation)/ (shows change of state)/(shows contrast)

21   中   zhong1/zhong4
      within/among/in/middle/center/while(doing something)/ during/China/Chinese, hit (the mark)

22   曰   yue1 to speak/to say

23   下   xia4   under/second (of two parts)/next (week, etc.)/lower/below/underneath/down(wards)/to decline/to go down/latter

24   于   yu2   (surname), in/at/to/from/by/than/out of

25   三   san1 three/3

26   得   de2/de/dei3
obtain/get/gain/proper/suitable/proud/contented/allow/permit/ ready/finished, a sentence particle used after a verb to show effect/ degree

or possibility, to have to/must/ought to/to need
to

27　在　zai4　(located) at/in/exist

28　年　nian2 year

29　我　wo3　I/me/myself

30　他　ta1　he/him

31　王　wang2　　king/Wang (proper name)

32　说　shui4/shuo1 persuade, to speak/to
say

33　事　shi4　matter/thing/item/work/affair

34　见　jian4/xian4　to see/to meet/to
appear (to be something)/to interview, appear

35　将　jiang1/jiang4　　(will, shall, "future
tense")/ready/prepared/to get/to use, a general

36　者　zhe3　-ist, -er (person)/person (who
does something)

37　去　qu4　to go/to leave/to remove

38   日   ri4   Japan/day/sun/date/day of the month

39   天   tian1   day/sky/heaven

40   州   zhou1 state/province/sub-prefecture

41   出   chu1   to go out/to come out/to occur/to produce/to go beyond/to rise/to put forth/to occur/to happen/ (a measure word for dramas, plays, or operas)

42   后   hou4   empress/queen/surname, back/behind/rear/afterwards/after/later

43   又   you4   (once) again/also/both... and.../again

44   自   zi4   from/self/oneself/since

45   此   ci3   this/these

46   个   ge4   (a general measure word)/individual

47   时   shi2   o'clock/time/when/hour/season/period

48   无   wu2   -less/not to have/no/none/not/to lack/un-

49　军　1-Jun　army/military/arms

50　太　tai4　highest/greatest/too (much)/very/extremely

51　这　zhe4/zhei4　this/these, this/these

52　与　yu2/yu3/yu4　(interrog. part.), and/to give/together with, take part in

53　月　yue4　moon/month

54　所　suo3　actually/place

55　家　jia1　furniture/tool, -ist/-er/-ian/home/family/a person engaged in a certain art or profession

56　如　ru2　as (if)/such as

57　知　zhi1　to know/to be aware

58　你　ni3　you

59　里　li3　inside/internal/interior, village/within/inside, Chinese mile/neighborhood/li, a Chinese unit of length = one-half kilometer/hometown

60 公 gong1 just/honorable (designation)/public/common

61 行 hang2/xing2/xing4 a row/profession/professional, all right/capable/competent/OK/okay/to go/to do/to travel/temporary/to walk/to go/will do, behavior/conduct

62 可 ke3 can/may/able to/certain(ly)/to suit/(particle used for emphasis)

63 使 shi3 to make/to cause/to enable/to use/to employ/messenger

64 到 dao4 to (a place)/until (a time)/up to/to go/to arrive

65 四 si4 four/4

66 至 zhi4 arrive/most/to/until

67 五 wu3 five/5

68 那 na3/na4/nei4 how/which, that/those, that/those

69 官 guan1 official/government

70 书 shu1 book/letter

71 生 sheng1 to be born/to give birth/life/to grow

72 小 xiao3 small/tiny/few/young

73 言 yan2 to speak/to say/talk/word

74 何 he2 carry/what/how/why/which

75 相 xiang1/xiang4 each other/one another/mutually, appearance/portrait/picture

76 兵 bing1 soldiers/a force/an army/weapons/arms/military/warlike

77 今 jin1 today/modern/present/current/this/now

78 都 dou1/du1 all/both (if two things are involved)/entirely (due to) each/even/already, capital city

79 南 nan2 south

80 山 shan1 mountain/hill

81 就 jiu4 at once/then/right away/only/(emphasis)/to approach/to move towards/to undertake

82 只 qi2/zhi1/zhi3 earth-spirit/peace, (a measure word, for birds and some animals, etc.)/single/only, M for one of a pair, only/merely/just/but, but/only

83 正 zheng1/zheng4 Chinese 1st month of year, just (right)/main/upright/ straight/correct/principle

84 前 qian2 before/in front/ago/former/previous/earlier/front

85 明 ming2clear/bright/to understand/next/the Ming dynasty

86 东 dong1east

87 着 zhao1/zhao2/zhe/zhu4/zhuo2 catch/receive/suffer, part. indicates the successful result of a verb/to touch/to come in contact with/to feel/to be affected by/to catch fire/to fall asleep/to burn, -ing part. (indicates an action in progress)/part. coverb-forming after some verbs, to make known/to show/to prove/to write/book/outstanding, to wear (clothes)/to contact/to use/to apply

88　门　men2
opening/door/gate/doorway/gateway/valve/switch/way to do something/knack/family/house/(religious) sect/school (of thought)/class/category

89　帝　di4　emperor

90　等　deng3 class/rank/grade/equal to/same as/wait for/await/et cetera/and so on

91　文　wen2
language/culture/writing/formal/literary

92　国　guo2　country/state/nation

93　百　bai3　hundred

94　西　xi1　west

95　心　xin1　heart/mind

96　安　an1　content/calm/still/quiet/to pacify/peace

97　然　ran2　correct/right/so/thus/like this/-ly

98　要　yao1/yao4
demand/ask/request/coerce,
important/vital/to want/to be going to/must

99　好　hao3/hao4　good/well, be fond of

100　入　ru4　to enter

Made in the USA
Las Vegas, NV
07 July 2021